Ring Out Wi

RING OUT WILD BELLS

A CELEBRATION OF CHRISTIAN VERSE

Chosen by Zenka
and Ian Woodward

Illustrated by Virginia Salter

HUTCHINSON
London Melbourne Auckland Johannesburg

Copyright © in this collection Zenka and Ian Woodward 1987
Copyright © Illustrations Virginia Salter 1987

First published in 1987 by Hutchinson Children's Books
An imprint of Century Hutchinson Ltd
Brookmount House, 62–65 Chandos Place, Covent Garden
London WC2N 4NW

Century Hutchinson Australia Pty Ltd
16–22 Church Street, Hawthorn, Melbourne, Victoria 3122

Century Hutchinson New Zealand Limited
32–34 View Road, PO Box 40–086, Glenfield, Auckland 10

Century Hutchinson South Africa (Pty) Ltd
PO Box 337, Bergvlei 2012, South Africa

Set in Garamond by BookEns, Saffron Walden, Essex
Printed and bound in Great Britain by Anchor Brendon Ltd,
Tiptree, Essex

British Library Cataloguing in Publication Data

Ring out wild bells: a celebration of Christian verse.
1. English poetry   2. Christian life in
literature
I. Woodward, Ian   II. Woodward, Zenka
821'.008'0382   PR1195.C48

ISBN 0-09-170390-5

Contents

To
the Reverend Gerald Drew,
Vicar of St Paul's Church,
Langleybury

St Paul's Church, Langleybury

Introduction

We have long felt the need for a collection of
poetry for children which proclaims the Christian
faith in all its drama, colour, inspiration and radiant
splendour. Here it is. We hope that these 'poems of
praise' afford as much enrichment, and provide as
many happy hours, as we ourselves have derived
while collecting them.

Zenka and Ian Woodward

In the beginning

God

It is the unimportant
who make all the din:
both God and the Accuser
speak very softly.

God never makes knots,
but is expert, if asked to,
at untying them.

Does God ever judge
us by appearances? I
suspect that He does.

W. H. Auden

God is born

The history of the cosmos
is the history of the struggle of becoming.
When the dim flux of unformed life
struggled, convulsed back and forth upon itself,
and broke at last into light and dark
came into existence as light,
came into existence as cold shadow,
then every atom of the cosmos trembled with
    delight.
Behold, God is born!
He is bright light!
He is pitch dark and cold!

And in the great struggle of intangible chaos
when, at a certain point, a drop of water began to
    drip downwards
and a breath of vapour began to wreathe up,
Lo again the shudder of bliss through all the atoms!
Oh, God is born!
Behold, he is born wet!
Look, he hath movement upwards! He spirals!

And so, in the great aeons of accomplishment and
    débâcle
from time to time the wild crying of every electron:
Lo! God is born!

When sapphires cooled out of molten chaos:
See, God is born! He is blue, he is blue, he is
    forever blue!
When gold lay shining threading the cooled-off
    rock:
God is born! God is born! bright yellow and ductile
    he is born.

When the little eggy amoeba emerged out of foam
    and nowhere
then all the electrons held their breath:
Ach! Ach! Now indeed God is born! He twinkles
    within.

When from a world of mosses and of ferns
at last the narcissus lifted a tuft of five-point stars
and dangled them in the atmosphere,
then every molecule of creation jumped and clapped
    its hands:
God is born! God is born perfumed and dangling
    and with a little cup!

Throughout the aeons, as the lizard swirls his tail
    finer than water,
as the peacock turns to the sun, and could not be
    more splendid,
as the leopard smites the small calf with a spangled
    paw, perfect,
the universe trembles: God is born! God is here!

And when at last man stood on two legs and
    wondered,
and there was a hush of suspense at the core of
    every electron:
Behold, now very God is born!
God himself is born!

And so we see, God is not
until he is born.

And also we see
there is no end to the birth of God.

D. H. Lawrence

I am God

I am God.
I caress the twisting trees with invisible fingers,
      Can you see me?
I wet the flowing rivers with a burning tongue,
      Can you hear me?
I tear open budding flowers with thorn-bloodied
  hands,
      Can you touch me?
Or are you as blind as my Son's hunters?
I see you share your silver – but what am I to do?
Unleash my mighty wrath of anger?
Break the trees, drain the water?
Crumble the dead Earth
          into the void of my Kingdom. . .
No, vultures of my mind, I shall watch,
Like I have done for so long, oh, so long.
Frustrated,
Exasperated,
Old,
I tremble as you fumble through your wooden
  words.
But I shall wait, and weep a little, as you destroy
My Utopia,
My dreams,
My body.
      The wall is infinite between us –
        You must break free.
Only then will you see me.
Only then will you hear me.
Only then will you touch me.
I am God.
I am you.
Denise Wright

12

The new Dial

In those twelve days let us be glad,
For God of his power hath all things made.
What are they that are but one?
What are they that are but one?
One God, one Baptism, and one Faith,
One Truth there is, the Scripture saith.

What are they that are but two?
Two Testaments, the old and new,
We do acknowledge to be true.

What are they that are but three?
Three Persons are in Trinity,
Which makes one God in unity.

What are they that are but four?
Four sweet Evangelists there are,
Christ's birth, life, death, which do declare.

What are they that are but five?
Five senses, like five kings, maintain
In every man a several reign.

What are they that are but six?
Six days to labour is not wrong,
For God himself did work so long.

What are they that are but seven?
Seven liberal arts hath God sent down,
With divine skill man's soul to crown.

What are they that are but eight?
Eight beatitudes are there given,
Use them right and go to heaven.

What are they that are but nine?
Nine Muses, like the heavens' nine spheres,
With sacred tunes entice our ears.

What are they that are but ten?
Ten statutes God to Moses gave,
Which, kept or broke, do spill or save.

What are they that are but eleven?
Eleven thousand virgins did partake,
And suffered death for Jesus' sake.

What are they that are but twelve?
Twelve are attending on God's Son;
Twelve make our Creed. The Dial's done.

Booth Haskell

All things bright and beautiful

All things bright and beautiful,
   All creatures great and small,
All things wise and wonderful,
   The Lord God made them all.

Each little flower that opens,
   Each little bird that sings,
He made their glowing colours,
   He made their tiny wings.

The purple-headed mountain,
   The river running by,
The sunset, and the morning,
   That brightens up the sky;

The cold wind in the winter,
  The pleasant summer sun,
The ripe fruits in the garden,
  He made them every one.

He gave us eyes to see them,
  And lips that we might tell,
How great is God Almighty,
  Who has made all things well.

Cecil Frances Alexander

All things dark and fearful

All things dark and fearful,
All humans big and strong,
All bombs loud and deadly;
Does the Lord God think it's wrong?

Each little flower that closes,
Each little bird that dies,
He made their fading colours,
That darken up the skies.

The purple-headed human,
With blood all running by,
The sunset and the morning,
That terrorize the sky.

He gave us guns to fight with
And arms to make our hell.
How great is God Almighty
Who has made all things well!

Lyndon Quinn

15

Now begin, on Christmas Day

Moonless darkness stands between.
Past, O past, no more be seen!
But the Bethlehem star may lead me
To the sight of him who freed me
From the self that I have been.
Make me pure, Lord: thou art holy;
Make me meek, Lord: thou wert lowly;
Now beginning, and alway:
Now begin, on Christmas Day.

Gerard Manley Hopkins

All in the morning

It was on Christmas Day,
And all in the morning,
Our saviour was born
And our heavenly king:
And was not this a joyful thing?
And sweet Jesus they called him by name.

It was on the Twelfth Day,
And all in the morning,
The Wise Men were led
To our heavenly king:
And was not this a joyful thing?
And sweet Jesus they called him by name.

It was on Holy Wednesday,
And all in the morning,
That Judas betrayed
Our dear heavenly king:
And was not this a woeful thing?
And sweet Jesus we'll call him by name.

It was on Good Friday,
And all in the morning,
They crucified our saviour,
And our heavenly king:
And was not this a woeful thing?
And sweet Jesus we'll call him by name.

It was on Easter Day,
And all in the morning,
Our saviour arose,
Our own heavenly king:
The sun and the moon they did both rise with him,
And sweet Jesus we'll call him by name.

Unknown

Nativity: blessed the babe

The lamb

Little lamb, who made thee?
Dost thou know who made thee?
Gave thee life, and bid thee feed
By the stream and o'er the mead;
Gave thee clothing of delight,
Softest clothing, woolly, bright;
Gave thee such a tender voice,
Making all the vales rejoice?
Little lamb, who made thee?
Dost thou know who made thee?

Little lamb, I'll tell thee,
Little lamb, I'll tell thee:
He is called by thy name,
For he calls himself a lamb.
He is meek, and he is mild;
He became a little child.
I a child, and thou a lamb,
We are called by his name.
Little lamb, God bless thee!
Little lamb, God bless thee!

William Blake

Hail the King of Glory

Before the paling of the stars,
  Before the winter morn,
Before the earliest cock-crow,
  Jesus Christ was born:
Born in a stable,
  Cradled in a manger,
In the world his hands had made
  Born a stranger.

Priest and king lay fast asleep
  In Jerusalem;
Young and old lay fast asleep
  In crowded Bethlehem;
Saint and angel, ox and ass,
  Kept a watch together,
Before the Christmas daybreak
  In the winter weather.

Jesus on his mother's breast
  In the stable cold,
Spotless lamb of God was he,
  Shepherd of the fold:
Let us kneel with Mary maid,
  With Joseph bent and hoary,
With saint and angel, ox and ass,
  To hail the King of Glory.

Christina Rossetti

19

Then gladly in the manger

Joseph   Take heart, the journey's ended:
        I see the twinkling lights,
    Where we shall be befriended
        On this the night of nights.

Mary   Now praise the Lord that led us
        So safe into the town,
    Where men will feed and bed us,
        And I can lay me down.

Joseph   And how then shall we praise him?
        Alas, my heart is sore
    That we no gifts can raise him,
        We are so very poor.

Mary   We have as much as any
        That on the earth do live,
    Although we have no penny,
        We have ourselves to give.

Joseph   Look yonder, wife, look yonder!
        A hostelry I see,
    Where travellers that wander
        Will very welcome be.

Mary   The house is tall and stately,
        The door stands open thus;
    Yet, husband, I fear greatly
        That inn is not for us.

Joseph   God save you, gentle master!
        Your littlest room indeed,
    With plainest walls of plaster,
        Tonight will serve our need.

Host	For lordlings and for ladies
	    I've lodging and to spare;
	For you and yonder maid is
	    No closet anywhere.

Joseph	Take heart, take heart, sweet Mary,
	    Another inn I spy,
	Whose host will not be chary
	    To let us easy lie.

Mary	O aid me, I am ailing,
	    My strength is nearly gone;
	I feel my limbs are failing,
	    And yet we must go on.

Joseph	God save you, hostess, kindly!
	    I pray you, house my wife,
	Who bears beside me blindly
	    The burden of her life.

Hostess	My guests are rich men's daughters,
	    And sons, I'd have you know!
	Seek out the poorer quarters,
	    Where ragged people go.

Joseph	Good sir, my wife's in labour, Some corner let us keep.
Host	Not I: knock up my neighbour, And as for me, I'll sleep.

Mary	In all the lighted city
	    Where rich men welcome win,
	Will not one house for pity
	    Take two poor strangers in?

Joseph	Good woman, I implore you, Afford my wife a bed.
Hostess	Nay, nay, I've nothing for you Except the cattle shed.

Mary	Then gladly in the manger
	   Our bodies we will house,
	Since men tonight are stranger
	   Than asses are and cows.

Joseph	Take heart, take heart, sweet Mary,
	   The cattle are our friends,
	Lie down, lie down, sweet Mary,
	   For here our journey ends.

Mary	Now praise the Lord that found me
	   This shelter in the town,
	Where I with friends around me
	   May lay my burden down.

Unknown

On Christmas morning

Villagers all, this frosty tide,
Let your doors swing open wide,
Though wind may follow, and snow beside,
Yet draw us in by your fire to bide;
    Joy shall be yours in the morning!

Here we stand in the cold and the sleet,
Blowing fingers and stamping feet,
Come from far away you to greet –
You by the fire and we in the street,
    Bidding you joy in the morning!

For ere one half of the night was gone,
Sudden a star has led us on,
Raining bliss and benison –
Bliss tomorrow and more anon,
    Joy for every morning!

Goodman Joseph toiled through the snow,
Saw the star over a stable low;
Mary she might not further go –
Welcome thatch, and litter below,
    Joy was hers in the morning!

And when they heard the angels tell
'Who were the first to cry Nowell?
Animals all, as it befell,
In the stable where they did dwell!
    Joy shall be theirs in the morning!'

Kenneth Grahame

A Christmas carol

The Christ-child lay on Mary's lap,
  His hair was like a light.
(O weary, weary were the world,
  But here is all aright.)

The Christ-child lay on Mary's breast,
  His hair was like a star.
(O stern and cunning are the kings,
  But here the true hearts are.)

The Christ-child lay on Mary's heart,
  His hair was like a fire.
(O weary, weary is the world,
  But here the world's desire.)

The Christ-child stood at Mary's knee,
  His hair was like a crown,
And all the flowers looked up at him,
  And all the stars looked down.

G. K. Chesterton

Three Kings came riding

Three Kings came riding from far away,
   Melchior and Gaspar and Baltasar;
Three Wise Men out of the East were they,
And they travelled by night and they slept by day,
   For their guide was a beautiful, wonderful star.

The star was so beautiful, large, and clear,
   That all the other stars of the sky
Became a white mist in the atmosphere,
And by this they knew that the coming was near
   Of the prince foretold in the prophecy.

Three caskets they bore on their saddle-bows,
   Three caskets of gold with golden keys;
Their robes were of crimson silk, with rows
Of bells and pomegranates and furbelows,
   Their turbans like blossoming almond-trees.

And so the Three Kings rode into the West,
   Through the dusk of night, over hill and dell,
And sometimes they nodded, with beard on breast,
And sometimes talked, as they paused to rest,
   With the people they met at some wayside well.

'Of the child that is born,' said Baltasar,
   'Good people, I pray you, tell us the news;
For we in the East have seen his star,
And have ridden fast, and have ridden far,
   To find and worship the King of the Jews.'

And the people answered, 'You ask in vain;
   We know of no king but Herod the Great!'
They thought the Wise Men were men insane,
As they spurred their horses across the plain,
   Like riders in haste, and who cannot wait.

And when they came to Jerusalem,
    Herod the Great, who had heard this thing,
Sent for the Wise Men and questioned them;
And said, 'Go down unto Bethlehem,
    And bring me tidings of this new king.'

So they rode away; and the star stood still,
    The only one in the grey of morn;
Yes, it stopped, it stood still of its own free will,
Right over Bethlehem on the hill,
    The city of David where Christ was born.

And the Three Kings rode through the gate and the
        guard,
    Through the silent street, till their horses turned
And neighed as they entered the great inn-yard;
But the windows were closed, and the doors were
        barred,
    And only a light in the stable burned.

And cradled there in the scented hay,
    In the air made sweet by the breath of kine,
The little child in the manger lay,
The child that would be King one day
    Of a kingdom not human but divine.

His mother, Mary of Nazareth,
    Sat watching beside his place of rest,
Watching the even flow of his breath,
For the joy of life and the terror of death
    Were mingled together in her breast.

They laid their offerings at his feet:
    The gold was their tribute to a king,
The frankincense, with its odour sweet,
Was for the priest, the paraclete,
    The myrrh for the body's burying.

And the mother wondered and bowed her head,
    And sat as still as a statue of stone;
Her heart was troubled yet comforted,
Remembering what the angel had said,
    Of an endless reign and of David's throne.

Then the Kings rode out of the city gate,
    With a clatter of hoofs in proud array;
But they went not back to Herod the Great,
For they knew his malice and feared his hate,
    And returned to their homes by another way.

Henry Wadsworth Longfellow

Not for Him

Not for Him a big white ambulance,
But a slow donkey.
Not for Him flashing blue lights,
But the star of Bethlehem.
Not for Him the white hospital wards,
But a cold stable.
Not for Him a nice warm cradle,
But a manger full of straw.
Not for Him fleecy babygros,
But plain swaddling bands.
Not for Him the Midwife, Nurse and Doctors,
But three simple shepherds.
Not for Him Auntie and Uncle from the North,
But three Kings from the East.
Not for Him a cuddly teddy bear,
But a shepherd boy's lamb.
Not for Him a silver coin in his palm,
But frankincense, myrrh and gold.
Not for Him a future in computers,
But the crown of Heaven.

Daniel Salcedo

3

Crucifixion, resurrection and ascension

Crucifixion to the world by the Cross of Christ
(*Galatians 6:14*)

When I survey the wondrous cross
Where the young Prince of Glory died,
My richest gain I count but loss,
And pour contempt on all my pride.

Forbid it, Lord, that I should boast
Save in the death of Christ, my God;
All the vain things that charm me most,
I sacrifice them to his blood.

See from his head, his hands, his feet,
Sorrow and love flow mingled down;
Did e'er such love and sorrow meet?
Or thorns compose so rich a crown?

His dying crimson like a robe
Spreads o'er his body on the tree,
Then am I dead to all the globe,
And all the globe is dead to me.

Were the whole realm of nature mine,
That were a present far too small;
Love so amazing, so divine,
Demands my soul, my life, my all.

Isaac Watts

The leaves of life

Oh it's all under the leaves and the leaves of life,
Where I saw maidens seven,
And it's one of those was Mary mild,
Was our king's mother from heaven.

Then I asked them what they were looking for,
All under the leaves of life.
'I am looking for sweet Jesus Christ,
To be our heavenly guide.'

'Go you down, go you down to yonder town,
As far as you can see,
And there you will find sweet Jesus Christ
With his body nailed to a tree.'

'Dear mother, dear mother, do not weep for me,
Your weeping does me harm,
But John may be a comfort to you
When I am dead and gone.'

There's a rose and a rose and a gentle rose,
The charm that grows so green.
God will give us grace in every mortal place
For to pray to our heavenly queen.

Simon Webster

Christ's resurrection and ascension

You humble souls that seek the Lord,
   Chase all your fears away;
And bow with rapture down to see
   The place where Jesus lay.

Thus low the Lord of life was brought,
   Such wonders love can do;
Thus cold in death that bosom lay,
   Which throbbed and bled for you.

But raise your eyes and tune your songs;
   The saviour lives again:
Not all the bolts and bars of death
   The Conqueror could detain.

High o'er the angelic bands he rears
   His once dishonoured head;
And through unnumbered years he reigns,
   Who dwelt among the dead.

With joy like his shall every saint
   His vacant tomb survey;
Then rise with his ascending Lord
   To realms of endless day.

Philip Doddridge

He is risen

He is risen, he is risen,
  Tell it with a joyful voice;
He has burst his three days' prison;
  Let the whole wide earth rejoice.
Death is conquered, man is free,
Christ has won the victory.

Cecil Frances Alexander

A rhyme for Shrove Tuesday

Snick, snock, the pan's hot,
We be come a-shrovin'.
Please to gie us summat,
Summat's better'n nothin':
A bit o'bread, a bit o'cheese,
A bit o'apple dumplin' please.

Unknown

Easter

On Easter Day the woods are wide awake
As into leaf the buds of winter break,
And skins are cast away by every snake,
And baby fish dart round in stream and lake,
And hazel boughs with dangling catkins shake.

Across the fields where high the young grass grows,
On hunting trips our padding tomcat goes,
And every orchard now with whiteness blows,
And I shall soon be wearing my new clothes;
On Easter Day the Lord of heaven rose.

Leonard Clark

32

The world itself keeps Easter Day

The world itself keeps Easter Day,
The Easter larks are singing;
And Easter flowers are out today,
And Easter buds are springing;
    Hallelujah, Hallelujah:
The Lord of all things lives anew,
And all his works are rising too.

There stood three Maries by the tomb,
On Easter morning early;
When day had scarcely chased the gloom,
And dew was white and pearly:
    Hallelujah, Hallelujah;
With loving but with erring mind,
They came the Prince of Life to find.

The world itself keeps Easter Day,
Saint Joseph's star is beaming;
Saint Alice has her primrose gay,
Saint George's bells are gleaming;
    Hallelujah, Hallelujah:
The Lord hath risen, as all things tell:
Good Christians, see you rise as well.

John Mason Neale

Rhyme for remembering the date of Easter

No need for confusion if we but recall
That Easter on the first Sunday after the full moon
    following the vernal equinox doth fall.

Justin Richardson

4

Praise to the holiest

Praise ye the Lord
(Psalm 150)

Praise ye the Lord.

Praise God in his sanctuary,
Praise him in the firmament of his power.

Praise him for his mighty acts,
Praise him according to his excellent greatness.

Praise him with the sound of the trumpet,
Praise him with the psaltery and harp.

Praise him with the timbrel and dance,
Praise him with stringed instruments and organs.

Praise him upon the loud cymbals,
Praise him upon the high-sounding cymbals.

Let every thing that hath breath praise the Lord.
Praise ye the Lord.

The Bible

Praise, my soul, the king of heaven

Praise, my soul, the king of heaven;
   To his feet thy tribute bring;
Ransomed, healed, restored, forgiven,
   Who like thee his praise should sing?
      Praise him, praise him,
   Praise the everlasting king.

Praise him for his grace and favour
   To our fathers in distress;
Praise him still the same for ever,
   Slow to chide, and swift to bless:
      Praise him, praise him,
   Glorious in his faithfulness.

Father-like he tends and spares us;
   Well our feeble frame he knows;
In his hands he gently bears us,
   Rescues us from all our foes:
      Praise him, praise him,
   Widely as his mercy flows.

Angels, help us to adore him,
   Ye behold him face to face;
Sun and moon, bow down before him;
   Dwellers all in time and space,
      Praise him, praise him.
   Praise with us the God of grace.

Henry Francis Lyte

The name of Jesus

How sweet the name of Jesus sounds
   In a believer's ear!
It soothes his sorrows, heals his wounds,
   And drives away his fear.

It makes the wounded spirit whole,
   And calms the troubled breast;
'Tis manna to the hungry soul,
   And to the weary rest.

Dear name! the rock on which I build,
   My shield and hiding-place,
My never-failing treasure filled
   With boundless stores of grace.

By thee my prayers acceptance gain,
   Although with sin defiled;
Satan accuses me in vain,
   And I am owned a child.

Jesus! my shepherd, husband, friend,
   My prophet, priest, and king;
My Lord, my life, my way, my end,
   Accept the praise I bring.

Weak is the effort of my heart
   And cold my warmest thought;
But, when I see thee as thou art,
   I'll praise thee as I ought.

Till then I would thy love proclaim
  With every fleeting breath;
And may the music of thy name
  Refresh my soul in death.

John Newton

All hail the power of Jesus' name

All hail the power of Jesus' name;
  Let angels prostrate fall;
Bring forth the royal diadem
  To crown him Lord of all.

Crown him, you morning stars of light,
  Who fixed this floating ball;
Now hail the strength of Israel's might,
  And crown him Lord of all.

Crown him, you martyrs of your God,
  Who from his altar call;
Extol the Stem of Jesse's Rod,
  And crown him Lord of all.

You seed of Israel's chosen race,
  You ransomed of the fall,
Hail him who saves you by his grace,
  And crown him Lord of all.

Hail him, you heirs of David's line,
  Whom David Lord did call,
The God incarnate, man divine,
  And crown him Lord of all.

Sinners, whose love can ne'er forget
  The wormwood and the gall,
Go, spread your trophies at his feet,
  And crown him Lord of all.

Edward Perronet

Praise to the holiest in the height¯
(from *The Dream of Gerontius*)

Praise to the holiest in the height,
  And in the depth be praise,
In all his words most wonderful,
  Most sure in all his ways.

Oh loving wisdom of our God!
  When all was sin and shame,
A second Adam to the fight
  And to the rescue came.

Oh wisest love! that flesh and blood,
  Which did in Adam fail,
Should strive afresh against the foe,
  Should strive and should prevail.

And that a higher gift than grace
  Should flesh and blood refine,
God's presence and his very self,
  And essence all-divine.

Oh generous love! that he who smote
  In man for man the foe,
The double agony in man
  For man should undergo.

And in the garden secretly,
  And on the cross on high,
Should teach his brethren, and inspire
  To suffer and to die.

Praise to the holiest in the height,
  And in the depth be praise,
In all his words most wonderful,
  Most sure in all his ways.   *John Henry Newman*

Hosanna to Christ

Hosanna to the royal son
   Of David's ancient line!
His natures two, his person one,
   Mysterious and divine.

The root of David, here we find,
   And offspring, are the same:
Eternity and time are joined
   In our Immanuel's name.

Blest he that comes to wretched man
   With peaceful news from heaven!
Hosannas, of the highest strain,
   To Christ the Lord be given.

Let mortals ne'er refuse to take
   The Hosanna on their tongues,
Lest rocks and stones should rise and break
   Their silence into songs.

Isaac Watts

Come, O Lord

Come like winter sunshine
Or the Christmas rose,
Come as frost on the lawn
Or the dancer's pose.

Come as sudden death
Or as a turning head,
Come as shyly as sleep
When words have been said.

Come as sorrow to joy,
Like a daughter's smile,
Or come with the warmth
Of a lover's profile.

Come as rain, come as sleet,
A smile in the street,
Come as noise or silence,
Come as peace or violence,
But come, Lord, come.

Cliff Ashby

5

Prayers: moments for reflection

A child's evening prayer

Ere on my bed my limbs I lay,
God grant me grace my prayers to say:
O God! preserve my mother dear
In strength and health for many a year;
And, O! preserve my father too,
And may I pay him reverence due;
And may I my best thoughts employ
To be my parents' hope and joy;
And O! preserve my brothers both
From evil doings and from sloth,
And may we always love each other
Our friends, our father, and our mother:
And still, O Lord, to me impart
An innocent and grateful heart,
That after my great sleep I may
Awake to thy eternal day! Amen.

Samuel Taylor Coleridge

An evening prayer

Glory to thee, my God, this night,
For all the blessings of the light:
Keep me, O keep me, king of kings,
Beneath thine own almighty wings.

O may my soul on thee repose,
And may sweet sleep mine eyelids close,
Sleep that shall me more vigorous make
To serve my God when I awake.

If in the night I sleepless lie,
My soul with heavenly thoughts supply;
Let no ill dreams disturb my rest,
No powers of darkness me molest.

All praise to thee in light arrayed,
Who light thy dwelling-place hast made;
A boundless ocean of bright beams
From thy all-glorious godhead streams.

Praise God, from whom all blessings flow,
Praise him, all creatures here below;
Praise him above, ye heavenly host:
Praise Father, Son and Holy Ghost.

Thomas Ken

A prayer to be said when you go to bed

O merciful God, hear this our request,
And grant unto us this night quiet rest.
Into your tuition, O Lord, do us take:
Our bodies sleeping, our minds yet may wake.
Forgive the offences this day we have wrought
Against you and our neighbour, in word, deed, and
    thought.
And grant us your grace henceforth to fly sin
And that a new life we may now begin.
Deliver and defend us this night from all evil,
And from the danger of our enemy, the Devil,
Which goes about seeking his prey
And by his craft whom we may betray.
Assist us, O Lord, with your holy sprite,
That valiantly against him we may ever fight;
And winning the victory, may lift up our voice,
And in your strength faithfully rejoice,
Saying, 'To the Lord be all honour and praise
For his defence both now and always!'

Francis Seager

Morning prayer

Now another day is breaking,
Sleep was sweet and so is waking.
Dear Lord, I promised you last night
Never again to sulk or fight.
Such vows are easier to keep
When a child is sound asleep.
Today, O Lord, for your dear sake,
I'll try to keep them when awake.

Ogden Nash

44

God bless me

I see the moon,
And the moon sees me;
God bless the moon,
And God bless me.

Unknown

Old shepherd's prayer

Up to the bed by the window, where I be lyin',
Comes bells and bleat of the flock wi' they two
    children's clack.
Over, from under the eaves there's the starlings
    flyin',
And down in yard, fit to burst his chain, yapping out
    at Sue I do hear young Mac.

Turning around like a falled-over sack
I can see team ploughin' in Whithy-bush field and
    meal carts startin' up road to Church-Town;
Saturday arternoon the men goin' back
And the women from market, trapin' home over the
    down.

Heavenly Master, I wud like to wake to they same
    green places
Where I know'd for breakin' dogs and follerin'
    sheep.
And if I may not walk in th' old ways and look on
    th' old faces
I wud sooner sleep.

Charlotte Mew

Gentle Jesus, meek and mild

Gentle Jesus, meek and mild,
Look upon a little child;
Pity my simplicity,
Suffer me to come to thee.

Fain I would to thee be brought,
Dearest God, forbid it not;
Give me, dearest God, a place
In the kingdom of thy grace.

Put thy hands upon my head,
Let me in thine arms be stayed,
Let me lean upon thy breast,
Lull me, lull me, Lord, to rest.

Hold me fast in thine embrace,
Let me see thy smiling face,
Give me, Lord, thy blessing give,
Pray for me, and I shall live.

Lamb of God, I look to thee,
Thou shalt my example be;
Thou art gentle, meek, and mild,
Thou wast once a little child.

Fain I would be as thou art,
Give me thy obedient heart;
Thou art pitiful and kind,
Let me have thy loving mind.

Let me, above all, fulfil
God my heavenly father's will,
Never his good spirit grieve,
Only to his glory live.

Thou didst live to God alone,
Thou didst never seek thine own,
Thou thyself didst never please:
God was all thy happiness.

Loving Jesus, gentle lamb,
In thy gracious hands I am;
Make me, saviour, what thou art,
Live thyself within my heart.

I shall then show forth thy praise,
Serve thee all my happy days;
Then the world shall always see
Christ, the holy child, in me.

Charles Wesley

The Ten Commandments

1   Have you no other gods but me,
2   And to no image bow your knee.
3   Take not the name of God in vain:
4   The sabbath day do not profane.
5   Honour your father and mother too;
6   And see that you no murder do.
7   Abstain from words and deeds unclean;
8   Nor steal, though you are poor and mean.
9   Bear not false witness, shun that blot;
10 What is your neighbour's covet not.

These laws, O Lord, write in my heart, that I
May in your faithful service live and die.

Unknown

The Lord is my shepherd
(*Psalm 23: a psalm of David*)

The Lord is my shepherd; I shall not want.
He maketh me to lie down in green pastures: he
    leadeth me beside the still waters.
He restoreth my soul: he leadeth me in the paths of
    righteousness for his name's sake.
Yea, though I walk through the valley of the shadow
    of death, I will fear no evil: for thou art with
    me; thy rod and thy staff they comfort me.
Thou preparest a table before me in the presence of
    mine enemies: thou anointest my head with oil;
    my cup runneth over.
Surely goodness and mercy shall follow me all the
    days of my life: and I will dwell in the house of
    the Lord for ever.

The Bible

6

Christmas bells

Ring Out, Wild Bells

Ring out, wild bells, to the wild sky,
  The flying cloud, the frosty light;
  The year is dying in the night;
Ring out, wild bells, and let him die.

Ring out the old, ring in the new,
  Ring, happy bells, across the snow;
  The year is going, let him go;
Ring out the false, ring in the true.

Ring out the grief that saps the mind,
  For those that here we see no more;
  Ring out the feud of rich and poor,
Ring in redress to all mankind.

Ring out a slowly dying cause,
  And ancient forms of party strife;
  Ring in the nobler modes of life,
With sweeter manners, purer laws.

Ring out the want, the care, the sin,
  The faithless coldness of the times;
  Ring out, ring out my mournful rhymes,
But ring the fuller minstrel in.

Ring out false pride in place and blood,
   The civic slander and the spite;
   Ring in the love of truth and right,
Ring in the common love of good.

Ring out old shapes of foul disease;
   Ring out the narrowing lust of gold;
   Ring out the thousand wars of old,
Ring in the thousand years of peace.

Ring in the valiant man and free,
   The larger heart, the kindlier hand;
   Ring out the darkness of the land,
Ring in the Christ that is to be.

Alfred, Lord Tennyson

Christchurch bells

Hark, the bonny Christchurch bells!
One, two, three, four, five, six;
They sound so sweet, so wondrous sweet,
They sound so merry, merry.

Hark, the first and second bell!
At every day goes four and ten,
Cries, 'Come, come, come, come, come to prayer
Or the verger stoops before the dean.'

Ting a ling ling, goes the small bell of ten,
To call the bearers home;
There's never a man will lose his can
Till he hears the mighty Tom.

Mary Croft

Note: Tom means 'church bell' in this poem

Peace and goodwill

On Christmas Day I sit and think,
Thoughts white as snow, and black as ink.
My nearest kinsman, turned a knave,
Robbed me of all that I could save.
When he was gone, and I was poor,
His sister yelped me from her door.

The Robin sings his Christmas song,
And no bird has a sweeter tongue.
God bless them all – my wife so true,
And pretty Robin Redbreast too.
God bless my kinsman, far away,
And give his sister joy this day.

W. H. Davies

Merry bells of yule
(from *In Memoriam*)

The time draws near the birth of Christ:
   The moon is hid, the night is still;
   The Christmas bells from hill to hill
Answer each other in the mist.

Four voices of four hamlets round,
   From far and near, on mead and moor,
   Swell out and fail, as if a door
Were shut between me and the sound.

Each voice four changes on the wind,
   That now dilate and now decrease,
   Peace and goodwill, goodwill and peace,
Peace and goodwill, to all mankind.

This year I slept and woke with pain,
   I almost wished no more to wake,
   And that my hold on life would break
Before I heard those bells again.

But they my troubled spirit rule,
   For they controlled me when a boy;
   They bring me sorrow touched with joy,
The merry, merry bells of yule.

Alfred, Lord Tennyson

Bells ringing

I heard bells ringing
Suddenly all together, one wild, intricate figure,
A mixture of wonder and praise
Climbing the winter-winged air in December.
Norwich, Gloucester, Salisbury, combined with
    York
To shake Worcester and Paul's into the old discovery
Made frost-fresh again.
I heard these rocketing and wound-remembering
    chimes
Running their blessed counterpoint
Round the mazes of my mind,
And felt their message brimming over with love,
Watering my cold heart,
Until, as over all England hundreds of towers
    trembled
Beneath the force of Christmas rolling out,
I knew, as shepherds and magi knew,
That all sounds had been turned into one sound,
And a single golden bell,
Repeating, as knees bowed, the name EMMANUEL.

Leonard Clark

Eddi's service (A.D. 687)

Eddi, priest of St Wilfrid
　In the chapel at Manhood End,
Ordered a midnight service
　For such as cared to attend.

But the Saxons were keeping Christmas,
　And the night was stormy as well.
Nobody came to service,
　Though Eddi rang the bell.

'Wicked weather for walking,'
　Said Eddi of Manhood End.
'But I must go on with the service
　For such as care to attend.'

The alter-lamps were lighted –
　An old marsh-donkey came,
Bold as a guest invited,
　And stared at the guttering flame.

The storm beat on at the windows,
　The water splashed on the floor,
And a wet, yoke-weary bullock
　Pushed in through the open door.

'How do I know what is greatest,
　How do I know what is least?
That is my father's business,'
　Said Eddi, Wilfrid's priest.

'But – three are gathered together –
　Listen to me and attend.
I bring good news, my brethren!'
　Said Eddi, of Manhood End.

And he told the ox of a manger,
  And a stall in Bethlehem,
And he spoke to the ass of a rider
  That rode to Jerusalem.

They steamed and dripped in the chancel,
  They listened and never stirred,
While, just as though they were bishops,
  Eddi preached them The Word.

Till the gale blew off on the marshes
  And the windows showed the day,
And the ox and the ass together
  Wheeled and clattered away.

And when the Saxons mocked him,
  Said Eddi of Manhood End,
'I dare not shut his chapel
  On such as care to attend.'

Rudyard Kipling

Goodwill to men, give us your money

It was Christmas Eve on a Friday,
  The shops was full of cheer
With tinsel in the windows,
  And presents twice as dear.
A thousand Father Christmases
  Sat in their little huts,
And folk was buying crackers
  And folk was buying nuts.

All up and down the country,
  Before the light was snuffed,
Turkeys they got murdered
  And cockerels they got stuffed,
Christmas cakes got marzipanned
  And puddin's they got steamed,
Mothers they got desperate
  And tired kiddies screamed.

Hundredweights of Christmas cards
  Went flying through the post,
With first-class postage stamps on those
  You had to flatter most.
Within a million kitchens,
  Mince pies was being made,
On everybody's radio,
  'White Christmas' it was played.

Out in the frozen countryside
  Men crept round on their own,
Hacking off the holly
  What other folks had grown.
Mistletoe in willow trees
  Was by a man wrenched clear,
So he could kiss his neighbour's wife
  He'd fancied all the year.

And out upon the hillside
  Where the Christmas trees had stood,
All was completely barren,
  But for little stumps of wood,
The little trees that flourished
  All the year were there no more,
But in a million houses
  Dropped their needles on the floor.

And out of every cranny, cupboard,
  Hiding place and nook,
Little bikes and kiddies' trikes
  Were secretively took.
Yards of wrapping paper
  Was rustled round about,
And bikes were wheeled to bedrooms
  With the pedals sticking out.

Rolled up in Christmas paper
  The Action Men were tensed,
All ready for the morning
  When their fighting life commenced.
With tommy guns and daggers,
  All clustered round about,
'Peace on Earth – Goodwill to Men'
  The figures seemed to shout.

The church was standing empty,
  The pub was standing packed,
There came a yell, 'Noel, Noel!'
  And glasses they got cracked.
From up above the fireplace
  Christmas cards began to fall,
And, trodden on the floor, said:
  'Merry Xmas to you all.'

Pam Ayres

On Christmas Day in the morning

There was a pig went out to dig,
On Christmas Day, Christmas Day,
There was a pig went out to dig
On Christmas Day in the morning.

There was a cow went out to plough,
On Christmas Day, Christmas Day.
There was a cow went out to plough
On Christmas Day in the morning.

There was a doe went out to hoe,
On Christmas Day, Christmas Day,
There was a doe went out to hoe
On Christmas Day in the morning.

There was a drake went out to rake,
On Christmas Day, Christmas Day,
There was a drake went out to rake
On Christmas Day in the morning.

There was a sparrow went out to harrow,
On Christmas Day, Christmas Day,
There was a sparrow went out to harrow
On Christmas Day in the morning.

There was a minnow went out to winnow,
On Christmas Day, Christmas Day,
There was a minnow went out to winnow
On Christmas Day in the morning.

There was a sheep went out to reap,
On Christmas Day, Christmas Day,
There was a sheep went out to reap
On Christmas Day in the morning.

There was a crow went out to sow,
On Christmas Day, Christmas Day,
There was a crow went out to sow
On Christmas Day in the morning.

There was a row went out to mow,
On Christmas Day, Christmas Day,
There was a row went out to mow
On Christmas Day in the morning.

Unknown

Christmas thoughts

Oh to be in India, now that winter's come,
Sweltering heat and lack of food,
But nothing can be done.

Oh to be in Africa, now that Christmas rings,
Poverty and homemade shacks.
How sweet the choirboy sings.

Oh to be in Poland, now for festive cheer,
Internment camps and martial law.
We'll go another year.

Oh to be in Belfast, now the snow has come,
Fights, explosions, massacres.
It doesn't sound much fun.

Oh to be in England, now that robins call,
Tinsel, baubles, shiny stars
The hypocrisy of it all.

Chloë Thomas

On Christmas Day

On Christmas Day it happened so,
Down in those meadows for to plough,
As he was ploughing all on so fast,
Up came sweet Jesus himself at last.

'O man, O man, why do you plough
So hard upon our Lord's birthday?'
The farmer answered him with great speed,
'For to plough this day I have got need.'

Now his arms did quaver through and through,
His arms did quaver, he could not plough,
For the ground did open and lose him in,
Before he could repent of sin.

His wife and children's out of place,
His beasts and cattle they're almost lost,
His beasts and cattle they die away,
For ploughing on old Christmas Day.
His beasts and cattle they die away,
For ploughing on our Lord's birthday.

Daniel Petrou

The first Nowell

The first Nowell

The first Nowell the angel did say
Was to certain poor shepherds in fields as they lay;
In fields where they lay keeping their sheep,
On a cold winter's night that was so deep.
Nowell, Nowell, Nowell, Nowell,
Born is the king of Israel.

They looked up and saw a star,
Shining in the East, beyond them far,
And to the earth it gave great light,
And so it continued both day and night.
Nowell, etc.

And by the light of that same star,
Three Wise Men came from country far;
To seek for a king was their intent,
And to follow the star wherever it went.
Nowell, etc.

This star drew nigh to the north-west,
O'er Bethlehem it took its rest,
And there it did both stop and stay,
Right over the place where Jesus lay.
Nowell, etc.

Then entered in those Wise Men three,
Full reverently upon their knee,
And offered there, in his presence,
Their gold, and myrrh, and frankincense.

Nowell, etc.

Then let us all with one accord,
Sing praises to our heavenly Lord,
That hath made heaven and earth of nought,
And with his blood mankind hath bought.

Nowell, etc.

Unknown

Away in a manger

Away in a manger, no crib for a bed,
The little Lord Jesus laid down his sweet head.
The stars in the bright sky looked down where he
    lay –
The little Lord Jesus asleep on the hay.

The cattle are lowing, the baby awakes,
But little Lord Jesus, no crying he makes.
I love thee, Lord Jesus! look down from the sky,
And stay by my side until morning is nigh.

Be near me, Lord Jesus; I ask thee to stay
Close by me for ever, and love me, I pray.
Bless all the dear children in thy tender care.
And fit us for heaven to live with thee there.

Unknown

Hark! the herald angels sing

Hark! the herald angels sing
Glory to the new-born king,
Peace on earth, and mercy mild,
God and sinners reconciled.
Joyful, all ye nations rise,
Join the triumph of the skies;
With the angelic host proclaim,
'Christ is born in Bethlehem.'
Hark! the herald angels sing
Glory to the new-born king.

Christ, by highest heaven adored,
Christ, the everlasting Lord,
Late in time behold him come,
Offspring of a virgin's womb,
Veiled in flesh the godhead see!
Hail, the incarnate deity!
Pleased as man with man to dwell,
Jesus, our Emmanuel.
Hark! the herald angels sing
Glory to the new-born king.

Hail, the heaven-born prince of peace!
Hail, the sun of righteousness,
Light and life to all he brings,
Risen with healing in his wings.
Mild he lays his glory by,
Born that man no more may die,
Born to raise the sons of earth,
Born to give them second birth.
Hark! the herald angels sing
Glory to the new-born king.

Charles Wesley

O come, all ye faithful

O come, all ye faithful
Joyful and triumphant,
O come ye, O come ye to Bethlehem;
Come and behold him,
Born the king of angels:
> *O come, let us adore him,*
> *O come, let us adore him,*
> *O come, let us adore him.*
> > *Christ the Lord!*

God of God,
Light of light,
Lo! He abhors not the virgin's womb;
Very God,
Begotten, not created:
> *O come, etc.*

Sing, choirs of angels,
Sing in exultation,
Sing, all ye citizens of heaven above;
'Glory to God
In the highest':
> *O come, etc.*

Yea, Lord, we greet thee,
Born this happy morning;
Jesus, to thee by glory given,
Word of the father,
Now in flesh appearing:
> *O come, etc.*

Translated from the Latin Adeste Fideles
by Canon Frederick Oakeley

While shepherds watched

While shepherds watched their flocks by night,
  All seated on the ground,
The angel of the Lord came down
  And glory shone around.

'Fear not,' said he; for mighty dread
  Had seized their troubled mind;
'Glad tidings of great joy I bring
  To you and all mankind.

'To you in David's town this day
  Is born of David's line
A saviour, who is Christ the Lord;
  And this shall be the sign.

'The heavenly babe you there shall find
  To human view displayed,
All meanly wrapped in swathing bands,
  And in a manger laid.'

Thus spake the seraph; and forthwith
  Appeared a shining throng
Of angels praising God, who thus
  Addressed their joyful song:

'All glory be to God on high,
  And to the earth be peace;
Goodwill henceforth from heaven to men
  Begin and never cease.'

Nahum Tate

8

Mercy, pity, peace and love

Walking with God

Oh! for a closer walk with God,
  A calm and heavenly frame;
A light to shine upon the road
  That leads me to the lamb!

Where is the blessedness I knew
  When first I saw the Lord?
Where is the soul-refreshing view
  Of Jesus and his word?

What peaceful hours I once enjoyed!
  How sweet their memory still!
But they have left an aching void
  The world can never fill.

Return, O holy dove, return,
  Sweet messenger of rest;
I hate the sins that made thee mourn,
  And drove thee from my breast.

The dearest idol I have known,
  Whate'er that idol be,
Help me to tear it from thy throne,
  And worship only thee.

So shall my walk be close with God,
  Calm and serene my frame;
So purer light shall mark the road
  That leads me to the lamb.

William Cowper

A child my choice

Let folly praise that fancy love, I praise and love
   that child
Whose heart no thought, whose tongue no word,
   whose hand no deed defiled.
I praise him most, I love him best, all praise and
   love is his;
While him I love, in him I live, and cannot live
   amiss.
Love's sweetest mark, laud's highest theme, man's
   most desired light.
To love him life, to leave him death, to live in him
   delight.
He mine by gift, I his by debt, thus each to other
   due,
First friend he was, best friend his is, all times will
   find him true.

Robert Southwell

God of love

This is the truth sent from above,
The truth of God, the God of love,
Therefore don't turn me from your door,
But hearken all both rich and poor.

The first thing which I do relate
Is that God did man create;
The next thing which to you I'll tell –
Woman was made with man to dwell.

And we were heirs to endless woes,
Till God the Lord did interpose;
And so a promise soon did run
That he would redeem us by his son.

And at that season of the year
Our blest redeemer did appear;
He here did live, and here did preach,
And many thousands did he teach.

Thus he in love to us behaved,
To show us how we must be saved;
And if you want to know the way,
Be pleased to hear what he did say.

Martin Ransome

The divine image

To Mercy, Pity, Peace, and Love
All pray in their distress;
And to these virtues of delight
Return their thankfulness.

For Mercy, Pity, Peace, and Love
Is God, our father dear,
And Mercy, Pity, Peace, and Love
Is Man, his child and care.

For Mercy has a human heart,
Pity a human face,
And Love, the human form divine,
And Peace, the human dress.

Then every man, of every clime,
That prays in his distress,
Prays to the human form divine,
Love, Mercy, Pity, Peace.

William Blake

Little Breeches

I don't go much on religion,
  I never ain't had no show;
But I've got a middlin' tight grip, sir,
  On the handful o' things I know.
I don't pan out on the prophets
  And free-will and that sort of thing –
But I b'lieve in God and the angels
  Ever sence one night last spring.

I come into town with some turnips,
  And my little Gabe come along,
No four-year-old in the county
  Could beat him for pretty and strong.
Peart and chipper and sassy,
  Always ready to blare and fight,
And I'd larnt him to chaw terbacker
  Jest to keep his milk-teeth white.

The snow come down like a blanket
  As I passed by Taggart's store;
I went in for a jug of molasses
  And left the team at the door.
They scared at something, and started –
  I heard one little squall –
And hell-to-split over the prairie
  Went team, Little Breeches, and all.

Hell-to-split over the prairie!
  I was almost froze with skeer;
But we rousted up some torches
  And sarched for 'em far and near.
At last we struck hosses and wagon,
  Snowed under a soft white mound,
Upsot, dead beat – but of little Gabe
  No hide nor hair was found.

And here all hope soured on me
    Of my fellow-critters' aid;
I jest flopped down on my marrow-bones,
    Crotch-deep in the snow, and prayed.
By this, the torches was played out,
    And me and Isrul Parr
Went off for some wood to a sheepfold
    That he said was somewhar thar.

We found it at last, and a little shed
    Where they shut up the lambs at night.
We looked in and seen them huddled thar,
    So warm and sleepy and white;
And thar sot Little Breeches and chirped,
    As peart as ever you see,
'I want a chaw of terbacker,
    And that's what the matter of me.'

How did he git thar? Angels.
    He could never have walked in that storm:
They jest scooped down and toted him
    To whar it was safe and warm.
And I think that saving a little child,
    And fotching him to his own,
Is a derned sight better business
    Than loafing around The Throne.

John Hay

First Thanksgiving of all

Peace and Mercy and Jonathan,
And Patience (very small),
Stood by the table giving thanks
The first Thanksgiving of all.
There was very little for them to eat,
Nothing special and nothing sweet;
Only bread and a little broth,
And a bit of fruit (and no tablecloth);
But Peace and Mercy and Jonathan
And Patience, in a row,
Stood up and asked a blessing on
Thanksgiving, long ago.

Thankful they were their ship had come
Safely across the sea;
Thankful they were for hearth and home,
And kin and company;
They were glad of broth to go with their bread,
Glad their apples were round and red,
Glad of mayflowers they would bring
Out of the woods again next spring.
So Peace and Mercy and Jonathan,
And Patience (very small),
Stood up gratefully giving thanks
The first Thanksgiving of all.

Nancy Byrd Turner

Our saviour's love

Here is a fountain of Christ's blood
Wide open set to drown our sins,
Where Christ stands with open arms
With mercy to invite you in.

For you will see his bleeding wounds
And hear him breathe forth dying groans.
He shed his rich redeeming blood
Only to do poor sinners good.

A crown of thorns, spit on with scorn,
His soul was pained and his flesh was torn,
With ragged nails through hands and feet
They nailed our rich redeemer sweet.

When all his precious blood was spent,
The thunder roared, the rocks were rent.
The richness of his precious blood
Did open graves and raise the dead.

The sun and moon in mourning went,
The sea did roar and the temples rent.
The earth did quake and the clouds did tumble
Which made hell shake and devils tremble.

Edmund Turner

O God, I love thee

O God, I love thee, I love thee –
Not out of hope of heaven for me
Nor fearing not to love and be
　In the everlasting burning.
Thou, thou, my Jesus, after me
　Didst reach thine arms out dying,
For my sake sufferedst nails and lance,
Mocked and marred countenance,
　Sorrows passing number,
　Sweat and care and cumber,
Yea and death, and this for me,
And thou couldst see me sinning:
Then I, why should not I love thee,
Jesu so much in love with me?
Not for heaven's sake; not to be
Out of hell by loving thee;
Not for any gains I see;
But just the way that thou didst me
I do love and I will love thee:
What must I love thee, Lord, for then? –
For being my king and God. Amen.

Gerard Manley Hopkins

74

Faith

How brittle are the piers
On which our faith doth tread.
No bridge below doth totter so,
Yet none hath such a crowd.

It is as old as God –
Indeed, 'twas built by him;
He sent his son to test the plank,
And he pronounced it firm.

Emily Dickinson

9
Wise words

God to be first served

Honour thy parents; but good manners call
Thee to adore thy God, the first of all.

Robert Herrick

Our Saviour's golden rule

Be you to others kind and true,
As you'd have others be to you;
And neither do nor say to men
Whate'er you would not take again.

Isaac Watts

A grace for children

What God gives, and what we take,
'Tis a gift for Christ his sake:
Be the meal of beans and peas,
God be thanked for those, and these:
Have we flesh, or have we fish,
All are fragments from his dish.
He his church save, and the king,
And our peace here, like a spring,
Make it ever flourishing.

Robert Herrick

Upon the swallow

This pretty bird, oh, how she flies and sings!
But could she do so if she had not wings?
Her wings bespeak my faith, her songs my peace;
When I believe and sing, my doubtings cease.

John Bunyan

Three little owls who sang hymns

There were three little owls in a wood
Who sang hymns whenever they could;
   What the words were about
   One could never make out,
But one felt it was doing them good.

Unknown

God made bees

Bees, bees of paradise,
Do the work of Jesus Christ,
Do the work that no man can.

God made bees,
Bees make honey;
God made men,
Men make money;
God made men
To harrow and to plough,
And God made the little boy
To holla off the crow –
   Holla, boys, holla, hip hip hurrah!

Unknown

Abou Ben Adhem

Abou Ben Adhem (may his tribe increase!)
Awoke one night from a deep dream of peace,
And saw, within the moonlight in his room,
Making it rich, and like a lily in bloom,
An angel writing in a book of gold.
Exceeding peace had made Ben Adhem bold,
And to the presence in the room he said,
    'What writest thou?' – The vision raised its head,
And with a look made of all sweet accord,
Answered, 'The names of those who love the Lord.'
    'And is mine one?' said Abou. 'Nay, not so,'
Replied the angel. Abou spoke more low,
But cheerly still; and said, 'I pray thee, then,
Write me as one that loves his fellow men.'
    The angel wrote, and vanished. The next night
It came again with a great wakening light,
And showed the names whom love of God had
        blest,
And lo! Ben Adhem's name led all the rest.

Leigh Hunt

Advice to a child

Dear child, these words which briefly I declare,
Let them not hang like jewels in thine ear;
But in the secret closet of thine heart,
Lock them up safe, that they may ne'er depart.

Give first to God the flower of thy youth;
Take scripture for thy guide, that word of truth;
Adorn thy soul with grace; prize wisdom more
Than all the pearls upon the Indian shore.

Be loving, patient, courteous, and kind:
So doing, thou shalt praise and honour find
Here upon earth; and when all-conquering death
Thy body shall dissolve, and stop thy breath,
Upon the golden wings of faith and love
Thy soul shall fly to paradise above.

Bernard Adams

My mother

Who taught my infant lips to pray,
And love GOD's holy book and day,
And walk in wisdom's pleasant way?

My mother.

And can I ever cease to be
Affectionate and kind to thee,
Who was so very kind to me,

My mother?

Ah, no! the thought I cannot bear,
And if GOD please my life to spare,
I hope I shall reward your care,

My mother.

When you are feeble, old and grey,
My healthy arm shall be your stay,
And I will soothe your pains away,

My mother.

And when I see you hang your head,
'Twill be my turn to watch your bed,
And tears of sweet affection shed,

My mother.

For could our father in the skies,
Look down with pleased or loving eyes,
If ever I could dare despise

My mother?

Ann Taylor

My mother's Bible

This book is all that's left me now,
   Tears will unbidden start;
With faltering lip and throbbing brow
   I press it to my heart.
For many generations past
   Here is our family tree;
My mother's hands this Bible clasped,
   She, dying, gave it me.

Ah! well do I remember those
   Whose names these records bear,
Who round the hearthstone used to close,
   After the evening prayer,
And speak of what these pages said
   In tones my heart would thrill!
Though they are with the silent dead,
   Here are they living still!

My father read this holy book
   To brothers, sisters, dear;
How calm was my poor mother's look,
   Who loved God's word to hear!
Her angel face – I see it yet!
   What thronging memories come!
Again that little group is met
   Within the walls of home.

You, truest friend man ever knew,
   Your constancy I've tried;
When all were false, I found you true,
   My counsellor and guide.
The mines of earth no treasures give
   That could this volume buy;
In teaching me the way to live,
   It taught me how to die. *George Pope Morris*

The Bible

The Bible is an antique volume,
Written by faded men
At the suggestion of holy spectres.
Subjects – Bethlehem;
Eden, the ancient homestead;
Satan, the brigadier;
Judas, the great defaulter;
David, the troubadour;
Sin, a distinguished precipice
Others must resist.
Boys that 'believe' are very lonesome,
Other boys are 'lost';
Had but the tale a warbling teller,
All the boys would come.
Orpheus' sermon captivated –
It did not condemn.

Emily Dickinson

Egocentric

What care I if good God be
If he be not good to me,
If he will not hear my cry
Nor heed my melancholy midnight sigh?
What care I if he created lamb,
And golden lion, and mud-delighting clam,
And tiger stepping out on padded toe,
And the fecund earth the blindworms know?
He made the sun, the moon and every star,
He made the infant owl and the baboon,
He made the ruby-orbed pelican,
He made all silent inhumanity,
Nescient and quiescent to his will,
Unquickened by the questing conscious flame
That is my glory amd my bitter bane.
What care I if skies are blue,
If God created gnat and gnu,
What care I if good God be
If he be not good to me?

Stevie Smith

10

Church and cleric

The church

This autumn day the new cross is set up
On the unfinished church, above the trees,
Bright as a new penny, tipping the tip
Of the elongated spire in the sunny breeze,
And is at ease;
Newcomer suddenly, calmly looking down
On this American university town.

Someone inside me sketches a cross – askew,
A child's – on seeing that stick crossed with a stick,
Some simple ancestor, perhaps, that knew,
Centuries ago when all were Catholic,
That this archaic trick
Brings to the heart and the fingers what was done
One spring day in Judaea to Three in One;

When God and Man in more than love's embrace,
Far from their heaven and tumult died,
And the holy dove fluttered above that place
Seeking its desolate nest in the broken side,
And Nature cried
To see Heaven doff its glory to atone
For man, lest he should die in time, alone.

I think of the Church, that stretched magnificence
Housing the crib, the desert, and the tree,
And the good Lord who lived on poverty's pence
Among the fishermen of Galilee,
Courting mortality,
And schooled himself to learn his human part:
A poor man skilled in dialectic art.

What reason for that splendour of blue and gold
For one so great and poor he was past all need?
What but impetuous love that could not hold
Its storm of spending and must scatter its seed
In blue and gold and deed,
And write its busy books on books of days
To attempt and never touch the sum of praise.

I look at the church again, and yet again,
And think of those who house together in hell,
Cooped by ingenious theological men
Expert to track the sour and musty smell
Of sins they know too well;
Until grown proud, they crib in rusty bars
The love that moves the sun and the other stars.

Yet fortune to the new church, and may its door
Never be shut, or yawn in empty state
To daunt the poor in spirit, the always poor.
Catholic, Orthodox, Protestant, may it wait
Here for its true estate.
All's still to do; roof, window and wall are bare.
I look, and do not doubt that he is there.

Edwin Muir

Parson Gray

A quiet home had Parson Gray,
  Secluded in a vale;
His daughters all were feminine,
  And all his sons were male.

How faithfully did Parson Gray
  The bread of life dispense –
Well 'posted' in theology,
  And post and rail his fence.

'Gainst all the vices of the age
  He manfully did battle;
His chickens were a biped breed,
  And quadruped his cattle.

No clock more punctually went,
  He ne'er delayed a minute –
Nor ever empty was his purse,
  When he had money in it.

His piety was ne'er denied;
  His truths hit saint and sinner;
At morn he always breakfasted;
  He always dined at dinner.

He ne'er by any luck was grieved,
  By any care perplexed –
No filcher he, though when he preached,
  He always 'took' a text.

As faithful characters he drew
  As mortal ever saw;
But ah! poor parson! when he died,
  His breath he could not draw!

Oliver Goldsmith

The Reverend Sabine Baring-Gould

The Reverend Sabine Baring-Gould,
   Rector (sometime) at Lew,
Once at a Christmas party asked,
   'Whose pretty child are you?'

(The Rector's family was long,
   His memory was poor,
And as to who was who had grown
   Increasingly unsure.)

At this, the infant on the stair
   Most sorrowfully sighed.
'Whose pretty little girl am I?
   Why, *yours*, papa!' she cried.

Charles Causley

Note: The Reverend Sabine Baring-Gould
(1834–1924) was Rector for forty-three years
at Lew Trenchard in Devon. He wrote many
books, including *The Lives of the Saints* in
fifteen volumes, and he is the author of the
hymn 'Onward, Christian soldiers' and of
'Now the day is over' – the last poem in this
anthology.

The bishop's mistake

The bishop glanced through his window pane
On a world of sleet, and wind, and rain,
When a dreary figure met his eyes
That made the bishop soliloquize.

And as the bishop gloomily thought
He ordered pen and pad to be brought,
Then 'Providence Watches' he plainly wrote
And pinned the remark to a five pound note.

Seizing his hat from his lordly rack
And wrapping his cloak around his back,
Across the road the bishop ran
And gave the note to the shabby man.

That afternoon was the bishop's 'at home'
When everyone gathered beneath his dome,
Curate and canon from far and near
Came to partake of the bishop's cheer.

There in the good old bishop's hall
Stood a stranger lean and tall,
'Your winnings, my lord' he cried. 'Well done
"Providence Watches", at ten to one.'

It is to be noted on Sunday next
The bishop skilfully chose his text,
And from the pulpit earnestly told
Of the fertile seed that returned tenfold.

Phoebe Powers

The bells of heaven

'Twould ring the bells of heaven
The wildest peal for years,
If parson lost his senses
And people came to theirs,
And he and they together
Knelt down with angry prayers
For tamed and shabby tigers
And dancing dogs and bears,
And wretched, blind pit-ponies,
And little hunted hares.

Ralph Hodgson

Parsons, priests and country vicars

Parsons, priests and country vicars
Love the food of city slickers,
They go to cafés with their vergers
For crinkle chips and cheesyburgers;
They shake on ketchup, spread on mustard,
And wash it down with prunes and custard!

Colin West

Blame the vicar

When things go wrong it's rather tame
To find we are ourselves to blame,
It gets the trouble over quicker
To go and blame things on the vicar.
The vicar, after all, is paid
To keep us bright and undismayed.
The vicar is more virtuous too
Than lay folks such as me and you.
He never swears, he never drinks,
He never *should* say what he thinks.
His collar is the wrong way round,
And that is why he's simply bound
To be the sort of person who
Has nothing very much to do
But take the blame for what goes wrong
And sing in tune at Evensong.

For what's a vicar really for
Except to cheer us up? What's more,
He shouldn't ever, ever tell
If there is such a place as hell,
For if there is it's certain he
Will go to it as well as we.
The vicar should be all pretence
And never, never give offence.
To preach on Sunday is his task
And lend his mower when we ask
And organize our village fêtes
And sing at Christmas with the waits
And in his car to give us lifts
And when we quarrel, heal the rifts.
To keep his family alive
He should industriously strive

In that enormous house he gets,
And he should always pay his debts,
For he has quite some pounds a week,
And when we're rude he should be meek
And always turn the other cheek.
He should be neat and nicely dressed
With polished shoes and trousers pressed,
For we look up to him as higher
Than anyone, except the Squire.

Dear people, who have read so far,
I know how really kind you are,
I hope that you are always seeing
Your vicar as a human being,
Making allowances when he
Does things with which you don't agree.
But there are lots of people who
Are not so kind to him as you.
So in conclusion you shall hear
About a parish somewhat near,
Perhaps your own or maybe not,
And of the vicars that it got.

One parson came and people said,
'Alas! Our former vicar's dead!
And this new man is far more "Low"
Than dear Old Reverend so-and-so,
And far too earnest in his preaching,
We do not really like his teaching,
He seems to think we're simply fools
Who've never been to Sunday Schools.'
That vicar left, and by and by
A new one came, 'He's much too "High",'
The people said, 'too like a saint,
His incense makes our Mavis faint.'
So now he's left and they're alone
Without a vicar of their own.
The living's been amalgamated
With one next door they've always hated.

John Betjeman

To the preacher

You suck in Good,
And spit out Sin
Just as you would
A spent grape-skin.

Light as a glove
You separate
The thing you love
From that you hate.

But this divorce
And glib conclusion
Is got, of course,
By their collusion.

In you contend
Both Good and Ill,
This will not end
In final spill

Of one or other:
God is not mocked, for
In steps Bother,
The King's Proctor.

W. R. Rodgers

93

The minister in the pulpit

The minister in the pulpit,
He couldn't say his prayers,
He laughed and he giggled,
And he fell down the stairs.
The stairs gave a crack,
And he broke his humpy back,
And all the congregation
Went 'Quack, quack, quack!'

Scottish nursery rhyme

The prayer of the little ducks

Dear God,
give us a flood of water.
Let it rain tomorrow and always.
Give us plenty of little slugs
and other luscious things to eat.
Protect all folk who quack
and everyone who knows how to swim.
    Amen.

Carmen Bernos de Gasztold (translated from the French by Rumer Godden)

A boy in church

'Gabble-gabble . . . brethren . . . gabble-gabble!'
   My window glimpses larch and heather.
I hardly hear the tuneful babble,
   Not knowing nor much caring whether
The text is praise or exhortation,
Prayer or thanksgiving or damnation.

Outside it blows wetter and wetter,
   The tossing trees never stay still;
I shift my elbows to catch better
   The full round sweep of heathered hill.
The tortured copse bends to and fro
In silence like a shadow-show.

The parson's voice runs like a river
   Over smooth rocks. I like this church.
The pews are staid, they never shiver,
   They never bend or sway or lurch.
'Prayer', says the kind voice, 'is a chain
That draws Grace down from heaven again.'

I add the hymns up over and over
   Until there's not the least mistake.
Seven-seventy-one. (Look! there's a plover!
   It's gone!) Who's that Saint by the Lake?
The red light from his mantle passes
Across the broad memorial brasses.

It's pleasant here for dreams and thinking,
   Lolling and letting reason nod,
With ugly, serious people thinking
   Prayer-chains for a forgiving God.
But a dumb blast sets the trees swaying
With furious zeal like madmen praying.

Robert Graves

Diary of a church mouse

Here among long-discarded cassocks,
Damp stools, and half-split-open hassocks,
Here where the vicar never looks
I nibble through old service books.
Lean and alone I spend my days
Behind this Church of England baize.
I share my dark forgotten room
With two oil-lamps and half a broom.
The cleaner never bothers me,
So here I eat my frugal tea.
My bread is sawdust mixed with straw;
My jam is polish for the floor.

 Christmas and Easter may be feasts
For congregations and for priests,
And so may Whitsun. All the same,
They do not fill my meagre frame.
For me the only feast at all
Is autumn's Harvest Festival,
When I can satisfy my want
With ears of corn around the font.
I climb the eagle's brazen head
To burrow through a loaf of bread.
I scramble up the pulpit stair
And gnaw the marrows hanging there.

 It is enjoyable to taste
These items ere they go to waste,
But how annoying when one finds
That other mice with pagan minds
Come into church my food to share
Who have no proper business there.
Two field mice who have no desire
To be baptized, invade the choir.

A large and most unfriendly rat
Comes in to see what we are at.
He says he thinks there is no God
And yet he comes . . . it's rather odd.
This year he stole a sheaf of wheat
(It screened our special preacher's seat),
And prosperous mice from fields away
Came in to hear the organ play,
And under cover of its notes
Ate through the altar's sheaf of oats.
A Low Church mouse, who thinks that I
Am too papistical, and High,
Yet somehow doesn't think it wrong
To munch through Harvest Evensong,
While I, who starve the whole year through,
Must share my food with rodents who
Except at this time of the year
Not once inside the church appear.

   Within the human world I know
Such goings-on could not be so,
For human beings only do
What their religion tells them to.
They read the Bible every day
And always, night and morning, pray,
And just like me, the good church mouse,
Worship each week in God's own house.

   But all the same it's strange to me
How very full the church can be
With people I don't see at all
Except at Harvest Festival.

John Betjeman

97

A young girl in the choir

There was a young girl in the choir,
Whose voice rose higher and higher,
   Till one Sunday night,
   It rose quite out of sight,
And they found it next day on the spire.

Unknown

Saints and sinners

All Saints

In a church which is furnished with mullion and
    gable,
  With altar and reredos, with gargoyle and groin,
The penitents' dresses are sealskin and sable,
  The odour of sanctity's eau-de-Cologne.
But only could Lucifer, flying from Hades,
  Gaze down on this crowd with its panniers and
    paints.
He would say, as he looked at the lords and the
    ladies,
  'Oh, where is All Sinners', if this is All Saints'?'

Edmund Yates

St Simeon

St Simeon could never be
A pillar of society;
And yet, for thirty years, upon
A pillar sat St Simeon.

Colin West

Antichrist

He walks, the enchanter, on his sea of glass,
Poring upon his blue inverted heaven
Where a false sun revolves from west to east.
If he could raise his eyes he would see his hell.
He is no spirit, nor a spirit's shadow,
But a mere toy shaped by ingenious devils
To bring discomfiture on credulous man.
He's the false copy where each feature's wrong,
Yet so disposed the whole gives a resemblance.
When he's in anguish smiles writhe on his lips
And will not stop. His imperturbable brow
Is carved by rage, not his but theirs that made him,
For he's a nothing where they move in freedom,
Knowing that nothing's there. When he forgives
It is for love of sin not of the sinner.
He takes sin for his province, knows sin only,
Nothing but sin from end to end of the world.
He heals the sick to show his conjuring skill,
Vexed only by the cure; and turns his cheek
To goad the furious to more deadly fury,
And damn by a juggling trick the ingenuous sinner.
He brings men from the dead to tell the living
That their undoing is a common fetch.
Ingeniously he postures on the tree
(His crowning jest), an actor miming death,
While his indifferent mind is idly pleased
That treason should run on through time for ever.
His vast indulgence is so free and ample
You well might think it universal love,
For all seems goodness, sweetness, harmony.
He is the Lie; one true thought, and he's gone.

Edwin Muir

Upon the weathercock

Brave weathercock, I see thou'lt set thy nose
Against the wind, which way soe'er it blows:
So let a Christian in any wise
Face Antichrist in each disguise.

John Bunyan

The sailor's carol

Noel! Noel! Noel! Noel!
A Catholic tale have I to tell!
And a Christian song have I to sing
While all the bells in Arundel ring.

I pray good beef and I pray good beer
This holy night of all the year,
But I pray detestable drink for them
That give no honour to Bethlehem.

May all good fellows that here agree
Drink Audit Ale in heaven with me,
And may all my enemies go to hell!
Noel! Noel! Noel! Noel!
May all my enemies go to hell!
Noel! Noel!

Hilaire Belloc

101

Hell

Hell is neither here nor there,
Hell is not anywhere,
Hell is hard to bear.

It is so hard to dream posterity
Or haunt a ruined century
And so much easier to be.

Only the challenge to our will,
Our pride in learning any skill,
Sustains our effort to be ill.

To talk the dictionary through
Without a chance word coming true
Is more than Darwin's apes could do.

Yet pride alone could not insist
Did we not hope, if we persist,
That one day hell might actually exist.

In time, pretending to be blind
And universally unkind
Might really send us out of our mind.

If we were really wretched and asleep
It would be then *de trop* to weep,
It would be natural to lie,
There'd be no living left to die.

W. H. Auden

I heard an angel singing

I heard an angel singing
When the day was springing,
'Mercy, Pity, Peace
Is the world's release.'

Thus he sung all day
Over the new mown hay,
Till the sun went down
And haycocks looked brown.

I heard a devil curse,
Over the heath and the furze,
'Mercy could be no more,
If there was nobody poor,

And pity no more could be
If all were as happy as we.'
At his curse the sun went down
And the heavens gave a frown.

And Miseries' increase
Is Mercy, Pity, Peace.

William Blake

12

A celestial journey

Jerusalem, my happy home

Jerusalem, my happy home,
  When shall I come to thee?
When shall my sorrows have an end,
  Thy joys when shall I see?

O happy harbour of the saints,
  O sweet and pleasant soil,
In thee no sorrow may be found
  No grief, no care, no toil.

There lust and lucre cannot dwell,
  There envy bears no sway;
There is no hunger, heat, nor cold,
  But pleasure every way.

Thy walls are made of precious stones,
  Thy bulwarks diamonds square;
Thy gates are of right orient pearl,
  Exceeding rich and rare.

Thy turrets and thy pinnacles
  With carbuncles do shine;
Thy very streets are paved with gold,
  Surpassing clear and fine.

Ah, my sweet home, Jerusalem,
  Would God I were in thee!
Would God my woes were at an end,
  Thy joys that I might see!

Thy gardens and thy gallant walks
   Continually are green;
There grow such sweet and pleasant flowers
   As nowhere else are seen.

Quite through the streets, with silver sound,
   The flood of life doth flow;
Upon whose banks on every side
   The wood of life doth grow.

There trees for evermore bear fruit,
   And evermore do spring;
There evermore the angels sit,
   And evermore do sing.

Our Lady sings *Magnificat*
   With tune surpassing sweet;
And all the virgins bear their part,
   Sitting about her feet.

Jerusalem, my happy home,
   Would God I were in thee!
Would God my woes were at an end,
   Thy joys that I might see!

Martin Derngate

Where is Jesus gone?

Dying! dying in the night!
Won't somebody bring the light
So I can see which way to go
Into the everlasting snow?

And 'Jesus'! Where is *Jesus* gone?
They said that Jesus always came.
Perhaps he doesn't know the House:
This way, Jesus – Let him pass!

Somebody run to the great gate
And see if Dollie's coming. Wait!
I hear her feet upon the stair.
Death won't hurt – now Dollie's here!

Emily Dickinson

Thee, God, I come from

Thee, God, I come from, to thee go,
All day long I like fountain flow
From thy hand out, swayed about
Mote-like in thy mighty glow.

What I know of thee I bless,
As acknowledging thy stress
On my being and as seeing
Something of thy holiness.

Once I turned from thee and hid,
Bound on what thou hadst forbid;
Sow the wind I would; I sinned:
I repent of what I did.

Bad I am, but yet thy child.
Father, be thou reconciled.
Spare thou me, since I see
With thy might that thou art mild.

I have life left with me still
And thy purpose to fulfil;
Yea a debt to pay thee yet:
Help me, sir, and so I will.

But thou bidst, and just thou art,
Me show mercy from my heart
Towards my brother, every other
Man my mate and counterpart.

Gerard Manley Hopkins

Heaven on high

O who will show me those delights on high?
           Echo: *I.*
Thou Echo, thou art mortal, all men know.
           Echo: *No.*
Wert thou not born among the trees and leaves?
           Echo: *Leaves.*
And are there any leaves that still abide?
           Echo: *Bide.*
What leaves are they? Impart that matter wholly.
           Echo: *Holy.*
Are holy leaves the echo then of bliss?
           Echo: *Yes.*
Then tell me, what is that supreme delight?
           Echo: *Light.*
Light to the mind: what shall the will enjoy?
           Echo: *Joy.*
But are there cares and business with the pleasure?
           Echo: *Leisure.*
Light, joy, and leisure; but shall they persever?
           Echo: *Ever.*

George Herbert

Going to heaven!

Going to heaven!
I don't know when –
Pray do not ask me how!
Indeed, I'm too astonished
To think of answering you!
Going to heaven!
How dim it sounds!
And yet it will be done
As sure as flocks go home at night
Unto the shepherd's arm!

Perhaps you're going too!
Who knows?
If you should get there first
Save just a little space for me
Close to the two I lost.
The smallest 'robe' will fit me
And just a bit of 'crown' –
For you know we do not mind our dress
When we are going home.

I'm glad I don't believe it,
For it would stop my breath,
And I'd like to look a little more
At such a curious Earth!
I'm glad they did believe it
Whom I have never found
Since the mighty autumn afternoon
I left them in the ground.

Emily Dickinson

God made a trance

Oh God made a trance on Sunday
All with his holy hand,
He made the sun fair on the moon
Like water on a dry land.

There's six good days all in a week
All for labouring man,
The seventh day to serve the Lord,
Both father and the son.

It's when you go to church, dear man,
Down on your knees down fall
And a-praying to our living Lord
For the saving of your soul.

For the saving of your soul, dear man,
Christ died along the road.
We shall never do for our saviour Christ
As he has done for we.

Three drops of our good saviour's blood
Were shed on Calvary.
We shall never do by our saviour Christ
As he has done by we.

Come teach your children well, dear man,
The whiles that you are here.
It will be better for your soul, dear man,
When you lies upon the bier.

Paul Clive

What God commands of me

I would have gone; God bade me stay:
  I would have worked; God bade me rest.
He broke my will from day to day,
  He read my yearnings unexpressed
    And said them nay.

Now I would stay; God bids me go:
  Now I would rest; God bids me work.
He breaks my heart tossed to and fro,
  My soul is wrung with doubts that lurk
    And vex it so.

I go, Lord, where thou sendest me;
  Day after day I plod and moil:
But, Christ my God, when will it be
  That I may let alone my toil
    And rest with thee?

Christina Rossetti

13

Tomorrow's story divine

Above the bright blue sky

There's a friend for little children
   Above the bright blue sky,
A friend who never changes,
   Whose love will never die;
Our earthly friends may fail us,
   And change with changing years,
This friend is always worthy
   Of that dear name he bears.

There's a home for little children
   Above the bright blue sky,
Where Jesus reigns in glory,
   A home of peace and joy;
No home on earth is like it,
   Nor can with it compare;
And everyone is happy,
   Nor could be happier there.

Albert Midlane

Sunday worship

Lord, how delightful 'tis to see
A whole assembly worship thee!
At once they sing, at once they pray;
They hear of heaven and learn the way.

I have been there and still would go:
'Tis like a little heaven below!
Not all my pleasure and my play
Shall tempt me to forget this day.

O write upon my memory, Lord,
The text and doctrines of thy word;
That I may break thy laws no more,
But love thee better than before.

With thoughts of Christ and things divine
Fill up this foolish heart of mine;
That, hoping pardon through his blood,
I may lie down and wake with God.

Isaac Watts

Song to my Lord on earth

My song is love unknown,
  My saviour's love to me;
Love to the loveless shown,
  That they might lovely be.
    O who am I,
    That for my sake
    My Lord should take
    Frail flesh and die?

He came from his blest throne,
  Salvation to bestow;
But men made strange, and none
  The longed-for Christ would know.
    But O, my friend,
    My friend indeed,
    Who at my need
    His life did spend!

Sometimes they strew his way,
  And his sweet praises sing,
Resounding all the day
  Hosannas to their king.
    Then 'Crucify!'
    Is all their breath,
    And for his death
    They thirst and cry.

Why, what hath my Lord done?
  What makes this rage and spite?
He made the lame to run,
  He gave the blind their sight:
    Sweet injuries!
    Yet they are these
    Themselves displease,
    And 'gainst him rise.

They rise, and needs will have
  My dear Lord made away;
A murderer they save,
  The Prince of Life they slay.
    Yet cheerful he
    To suffering goes,
    That he his foes
    From thence might free.

In life no house, no home,
  My Lord on earth might have;
In death no friendly tomb,
  But what a stranger gave.
    What may I say?
    Heaven was his home;
    But mine the tomb
    Wherein he lay.

Here might I stay and sing,
  No story so divine;
Never was love, dear king,
  Never was grief like thine!
    This is my friend,
    In whose sweet praise
    I all my days
    Could gladly spend.

Samuel Crossman

The man that lives

The man that lives must learn to die,
Christ will no longer stay.
Our time is short, death's near at hand
To take our lives away.

What are our lives that we must live
And what's our carcass then?
It's food for worms to feed upon,
Christ knows the time and when.

Our lives are like the grass, O Lord,
Like flowers in the field.
So welcome death, praise you the Lord,
Willing I am to yield.

Now we must die and leave this world
Which we have lived in,
Nothing but our poor winding-sheet
To wrap our bodies in.

Happy the man that never swears
Against his living Lord,
And never took God's name in vain
At any trifling word.

When shall we see that happy heaven,
That blessed resting place,
Where we like angels then shall feed
Upon God's royal grace?

Christopher Conrad

The question of Jesus?

At least to pray is left, is left,
Oh Jesus in the air;
I know not which thy chamber is:
I'm knocking everywhere.
Thou settest earthquake in the south
And maelstrom in the sea;
Say, Jesus Christ of Nazareth,
Hast thou no arm for me?

Emily Dickinson

The question of God?

God. A king? An emperor? How do you define it?
A tired old man with the world at his feet?
A long white beard and a kind old face?
God, what do you think of your human race?
You invented it, so they say,
Do you regret it in any way?
What do you think of evil and sin,
And the world that I'm growing up in?
God, can you cry, can you weep?
Do you laugh? – or have nightmares in your sleep?
What do you do all day? How do you fill your time?
Or do you just invent another life – commit another
    crime?
Can't you see the sufferers everywhere,
Or are you short-sighted? Or don't you care?
Do you see the children and their eyes filled with
    moisture,
And their gawky faces and their awkward posture?
Do you see the mass murders and the world full of
    blood?
Or can't you see beyond the church and its love?

I can't understand you, God. It's your creation,
Didn't you want a pure and gentle nation?
Didn't you want peace and tranquillity –
Or did you mean to have evil and impurity?

God! Are you there, listening to me?
Or am I just another voice, another silent plea?
Do you know what is happening on the land?
Can you see it from where you stand?

They're going to ruin your world, blow it all up.
Just one press on a button and the world will erupt.
You'll be out of a job, God. What will you do then?
Are you just going to begin all over again?

Rebecca Poole

The Garden of Love

I went to the Garden of Love,
And saw what I never had seen:
A chapel was built in the midst,
Where I used to play on the green.

And the gates of this chapel were shut,
And 'Thou shalt not' writ over the door;
So I turned to the Garden of Love
That so many sweet flowers bore.

And I saw it was filled with graves,
And tombstones where flowers should be;
And priests in black gowns were walking their
    rounds,
And binding with briars my joys and desires.

William Blake

There is a green hill

There is a green hill far away,
  Without a city wall,
Where the dear Lord was crucified,
  Who died to save us all.

We may not know, we cannot tell
  What pains he had to bear;
But we believe it was for us,
  He hung and suffered there.

He died that we might be forgiven,
  He died to make us good,
That we might go at last to heaven,
  Saved by his precious blood.

There was no other good enough
  To pay the price of sin,
He only could unlock the gate
  Of heaven, and let us in.

O dearly, dearly has he loved,
  And we must love him too,
And trust in his redeeming blood,
  And try his works to do.

Cecil Frances Alexander

Conviction

Christ died for God and me
Upon the crucifixion tree
For God a spoken word
For me a sword
For God a hymn of praise
For me eternal days
For God an explanation
For me salvation.

Stevie Smith

Heaven's gate

I give you the end of a golden string,
    Only wind it into a ball,
It will lead you in at heaven's gate
    Built in Jerusalem's wall.

William Blake

Hymnus

God be in my head
    And in my understanding,
God be in mine eyes
    And in my looking,
God be in my mouth
    And in my speaking,
God be in my heart
    And in my thinking,
God be at mine end
    And at my departing. Amen!

Unknown

Now the day is over

Now the day is over
  Night is drawing nigh,
Shadows of the evening
  Steal across the sky.

Now the darkness gathers,
  Stars begin to peep,
Birds and beasts and flowers
  Soon will be asleep.

Jesu, give the weary
  Calm and sweet repose;
With thy tenderest blessing
  May our eyelids close.

Grant to little children
  Visions bright of thee;
Guard the sailors tossing
  On the deep blue sea.

Comfort every sufferer
  Watching late in pain;
Those who plan some evil
  From their sin restrain.

Through the long night-watches
  May thine angels spread
Their white wings above me,
  Watching round my bed.

When the morning wakens,
  Then may I arise
Pure and fresh and sinless
  In thy holy eyes.

Glory to the father,
  Glory to the son,
And to thee, blest spirit,
  Whilst all ages run.

Sabine Baring-Gould

Index of first lines

Acknowledgments

The compilers and publishers would like to thank the following for permission to use copyright material in this collection. The publishers have made every effort to contact the copyright holders but there are a few cases where it has not been possible to do so. We would be grateful to hear from anyone who can enable us to contact them so the omission can be corrected at the first opportunity.

Pam Ayres for 'Goodwill to Men, Give Us Your Money' from *Some of Me Poetry* by Pam Ayres (Galaxy Records)

Cadbury Limited for 'The Question of God?' by Rebecca Poole, 'Christmas Thoughts' by Chloe Thomas, 'Not for Him' by Daniel Salcedo and 'All Things Dark and Fearful' by Lyndon Quinn from *Cadbury's First Book of Children's Poetry* (Beaver Books) and 'I am God' by Denise Wright from *Cadbury's Third Book of Children's Poetry* (Beaver Books)

Jonathan Cape Limited, on behalf of The Executors of the W. H. Davies Estate, for 'Peace and Goodwill' from *The Complete Poems of W. H. Davies*

Lucy Rodgers Cohen, and Campbell Thomson & McLaughlin Limited, for 'To the Preacher' from *The Collected Poems of W. R. Rodgers* (Oxford University Press) © W. R. Rodgers 1941

Curtis Brown Limited, London, on behalf of the Estate of Ogden Nash, for 'Morning Prayer' from *The New Nutcracker Suite and Other Innocent Verse* by Ogden Nash © Ogden Nash

Dobson Books Limited for 'Bells Ringing' from *Singing in the Streets* by Leonard Clark and for 'Easter' from *Collected Poems and Verse for Children* by Leonard Clark

Gerald Duckworth & Company Limited for 'The Sailor's Carol' from *The Complete Verse of Hilaire Belloc*

Faber and Faber Limited for 'God' (three extracts from 'Shorts II') and 'Hell' from *Collected Poems* by W. H. Auden and for 'The Church' and 'Antichrist' from *The Collected Poems of Edwin Muir*